Gun Education and Safety

GUN SPORTS

BRIAN KEVIN

ABDO Publishing Company

visit us at
www.abdopublishing.com

Published by ABDO Publishing Company, PO Box 398166, Edina, MN 55439.
Copyright © 2012 by Abdo Consulting Group, Inc. International copyrights reserved in all
countries. No part of this book may be reproduced in any form without written permission from the
publisher. The Checkerboard Library™ is a trademark and logo of ABDO Publishing Company.

Printed in the United States of America, North Mankato, Minnesota.
112011
012012

 PRINTED ON RECYCLED PAPER

Cover Photo: Getty Images
Interior Photos: Alamy pp. 7, 9, 16, 18, 26; AP Images pp. 4, 5; Corbis p. 23; Getty Images pp. 11,
    13, 14–15, 17, 21, 22, 29; Glow Images p. 6; iStockphoto pp. 8, 10, 17, 20, 28;
    Neil Klinepier p. 19; Thinkstock pp. 13, 24–25; Wikimedia Commons p. 27

Series Coordinator: Megan M. Gunderson
Editors: Megan M. Gunderson, BreAnn Rumsch
Art Direction: Neil Klinepier

Library of Congress Cataloging-in-Publication Data

Kevin, Brian, 1980-
  Gun sports / Brian Kevin.
      p. cm. -- (Gun education and safety)
  Includes index.
  ISBN 978-1-61783-317-5
  1. Shooting--Juvenile literature. I. Title.
  GV1153.K48 2012
  799.31--dc23
                        2011031434

CONTENTS

Bull's-Eye! 4

Spears to Guns. 6

Range Gear 8

Target Shooting 12

Shotgun Sports 16

Biathlon. 20

Pentathlon. .22

Targeting the Past 24

Concentrate!. 28

Glossary 30

Web Sites 31

Index. 32

Bull's-Eye!

Like any sport, gun sports are a great way to meet people and improve focus and confidence.

It had been a long afternoon at the shooting range. Tim's arms were tired. His rifle felt heavy after lots of target practice! But the shooting match was tomorrow. It was Tim's first, and he wanted to be ready.

Tim looked down the range at his paper target. Nine rings circled smaller and smaller around the bull's-eye. Tomorrow,

all the competitors would line up here. They would look at their own targets and take aim.

After the match, everyone would relax. They would eat hot dogs and tell jokes in the clubhouse. But Tim knew that the match would be tense and quiet. Aiming a rifle takes a lot of concentration.

Tim adjusted his safety glasses. He put his rifle to his shoulder, took a breath, and relaxed his muscles. Then he aimed at his target. When he pulled the **trigger**, there was a pop.

Tim felt good about his shot. He was calm and had taken good aim. When he was sure the range was clear, he picked up his target. There was a clean hole in the center. Bull's-eye!

People have aimed at targets for sport since ancient times. Spear throwing and archery were popular in Europe and Asia. During the Middle Ages, **marksmanship** became a social sport. Shooting clubs first appeared in the 1200s in Europe.

Star shooter Annie Oakley could hit a dime tossed into the air!

By the 1500s, club matches were public celebrations. In fact, they were often held on holidays. Competitors aimed their bows and muskets at painted wooden targets. Sometimes the winner's prize was gold.

In the 1700s, US frontiersmen held shooting contests called "rifle frolics" or "turkey shoots." They shot at targets to win prizes such as food, including turkey!

As firearms improved, shooting matches became more formal. By the 1800s, they sometimes attracted thousands of spectators. In 1898, one

shooting festival in New York awarded $25,000 in cash prizes. That's a fortune in today's dollars!

From the very beginning, shooting sports were also ways to practice military **techniques** and hunting. In the 1800s, sharpshooters like Annie Oakley shot in trap contests. These used glass balls filled with feathers to imitate bird hunting. Later, shooters aimed at disks called clay pigeons.

Exhibitions such as Buffalo Bill's Wild West show increased public interest in shooting sports. Today, rifle, shotgun, and pistol competitions remain popular. Shooting events are even part of the Olympic Games. And, they take place in towns across the world.

Range Gear

Unlike the informal contests of the past, today's shooting sports usually take place at shooting ranges. These are special areas for firearms practice. Many have both indoor and outdoor ranges. People visit them to practice with rifles, pistols, or shotguns.

The area people aim and shoot from is called the firing point. Behind the targets is a backstop. This stops bullets. Backstops are often made from dirt or steel bullet traps. They are an important safety feature for everyone on the range.

The shooting range is a great place to learn about gun safety.

Targets for pistols and rifles are usually sheets of paper. Their size varies with the distance from the firing point. In shotgun sports such as trapshooting, the targets are clay pigeons. Machines called traps launch these disks into the air. The soaring disks mimic flying birds.

All shooters must pay attention to what is behind their targets.

Earplugs

At the range, shooters always wear proper safety gear. Eye protection is required. Most shooters wear glasses made specifically for shooting. These have strong lenses to protect the eyes from flying objects.

The lenses also help improve performance. They reduce glare. And, they come in different colors. So, shooters can see well in different lighting.

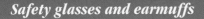
Safety glasses and earmuffs

Some safety glasses have added features. They may have shields on the sides called blinkers. These help block wind and other distractions.

Blinkers

Earplugs and earmuffs protect the shooter's hearing. Some electronic earmuffs have special features. They muffle very loud gun blasts. But they allow shooters to hear quieter sounds, such as nearby conversation.

Target Shooting

Target shooting comes in many different forms. It can be hard to keep track of all the options! Yet shooting sports are defined by three important questions. What weapon is used? What is the distance to the target? And, what is the shooter's position?

Various organizations oversee the different shooting sports. These groups establish rules and organize events. One important organization is USA Shooting. It oversees Olympic shooting sports.

In the Summer Olympics alone, there are 15 different shooting events. One is the 10-meter (33-ft) air pistol competition. For this event, the shooter fires from a standing position. He or she aims at a target that is 10 meters away.

In the 50-meter (164-ft) rifle **prone** competition, the shooter lays on the ground. He or she shoots at a target that is 50 meters away.

These events are scored according to where a shooter hits the target. A perfect bull's-eye scores ten points. Each ring away from the bull's-eye is worth one less point. In most target sports, the target has ten rings. So, the outer ring is worth only one point.

The exact size and design of a target depends on the weapon, distance, and event. Major events may use electronic targets instead of paper targets.

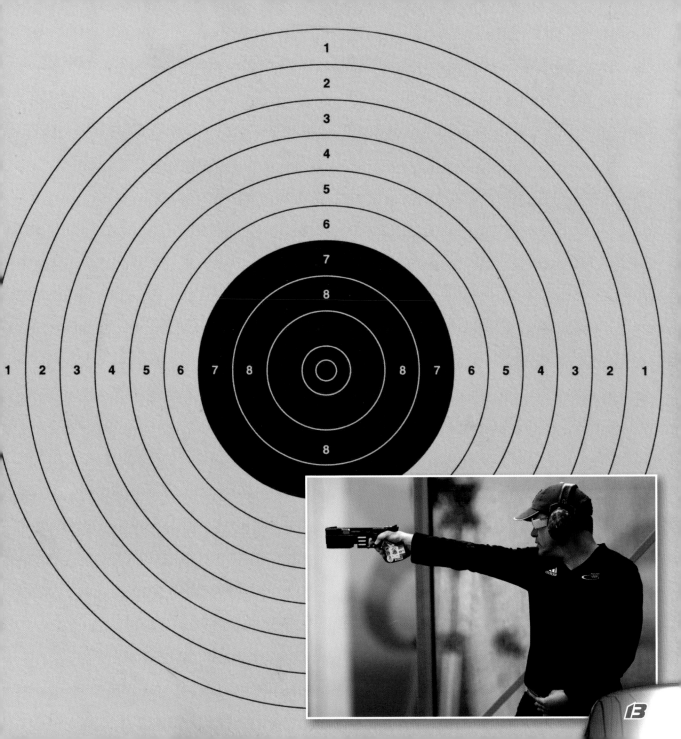

The type of shooting event also determines how many shots an athlete fires. In the Olympics, shooters in the men's 50-meter rifle **prone** event take 60 shots.

The combined points from all 60 shots make their scores before the final round. So, hitting the target's eight-point ring all 60 times is worth 480 points. Then, shooters move on to a final round. There, they score additional points.

Another Olympic event is the 25-meter (82-ft) rapid fire pistol. Shooters fire at 50-centimeter (20-in) targets. This event

has a special challenge. The targets are only visible for a few seconds! So, competitors have to be fast and precise.

Outside the Olympics, there are a variety of other target-shooting events. Some use special targets. For example, **silhouette** shooting involves firing at metal cutouts shaped like animals.

Other sports focus on shooting great distances. Organizations such as the International Confederation of Fullbore Rifle Associations oversee these sports. Talented shooters can join the US Long Range Rifle Teams. These athletes shoot at targets as far as 1,000 yards (914 m) away!

Shotgun Sports

A launching machine, or trap

Some athletes prefer the excitement of shotgun sports. These use clay pigeons as moving targets! The three main shotgun sports are trapshooting, skeet shooting, and sporting clays.

For each sport, launching machines throw the targets into the air. Shooters stand at different firing points called stations. Each shotgun sport uses different positions for launchers and stations.

In trapshooting contests, there are five stations at which a shooter stands. The stations are arranged next to one another in a line. Launching machines are positioned in front of the row of stations. When the shooter yells "pull!" they fire one or two clays.

The targets travel away from the shooter. In some events, the shooter already knows which direction the targets will go.

In others they're launched at **random** angles. So, it's hard to predict where to aim.

The flying disks are also very fast. In the Olympics, they zoom out of the traps at up to 65 miles per hour (105 km/h)! Shooters get one point for each target they hit.

Clay pigeons must be strong enough to be launched. But, they must break easily when shot.

Skeet shooting is a little different from trapshooting. In skeet, there are eight stations. Seven are arranged in a half circle. The eighth station is up front in the middle. The shooter moves from station to station.

The launchers are in two "houses" on either side of the range. Together, they fire one or two clay pigeons. The disks fly from the shooter's left or right. One house is higher than the other, so the targets start at different heights.

In skeet shooting, targets are always launched the same way. It's not **random** like it can be in trap. The challenge in skeet shooting comes from mastering the different angles of each station. Different types of shotguns can also be used.

The third shotgun sport is sporting clays. Shooters visit five or more

Golfers move from hole to hole on a golf course. Similarly, shooters move from station to station on a sporting clays course.

stations on a sporting clays course. Every station has its own launching machines. And at each station, they're located in a different place. This adds to the challenge!

Sometimes, two clays will be fired at the same time. Some fly away from the shooter. Others fly from left to right. That way, the targets imitate different types of birds.

Sporting clays is the only one of the three shotgun sports without an Olympic event. But it is a great way to practice using a shotgun. And walking between stations is good exercise, too!

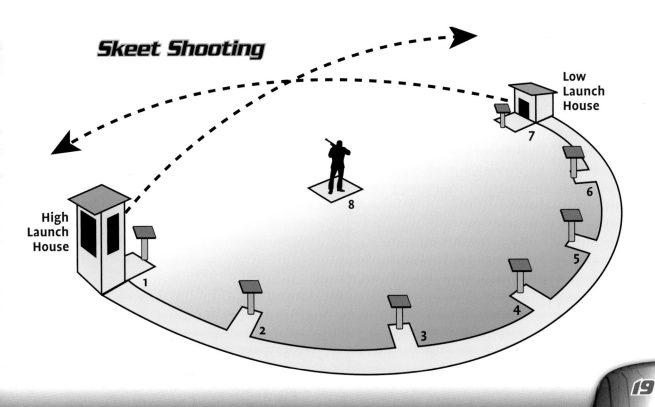

Skeet Shooting

Low Launch House

High Launch House

8

7

6

5

4

3

2

1

Biathlon

Some gun sports combine shooting with other athletic activities. These sports often have roots in history. One example is biathlon.

This sport combines shooting and skiing. It is very popular in Europe, where it began. The sport is based on the historical training of Scandinavian soldiers. The first recorded competition took place in 1767!

Today's biathletes carry their rifles on their backs as they cross-country ski around a track. After a certain distance, they stop

Racers shoot in two positions, standing up and lying down.

to shoot at five targets. When they're done shooting, they ski some more.

For each target athletes miss, there is a penalty. Depending on the race, a minute may be added to their time. Or, they may have to ski an extra distance.

In different versions of the sport, racers ski longer distances and shoot more times. Whatever the race, fast skiing makes muscles tired and hearts race. So, it is hard to aim the rifle steadily. Biathlon requires strength and steady nerves.

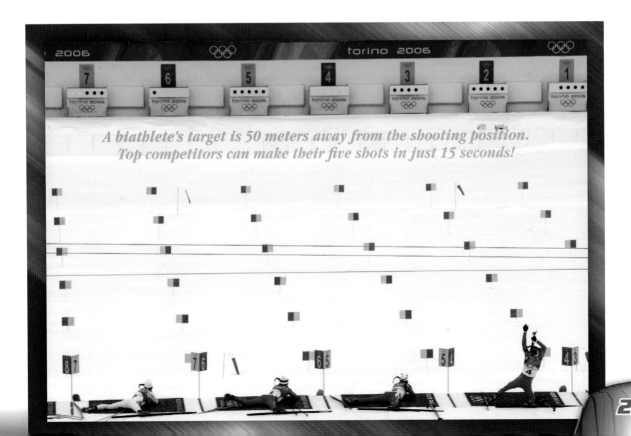

A biathlete's target is 50 meters away from the shooting position. Top competitors can make their five shots in just 15 seconds!

Pentathlon

Pentathletes shoot and run three times each during the race.

The wintertime biathlon combines two sports. But at the Summer Olympics, athletes compete in modern pentathlon. It consists of five sports! These are fencing, swimming, horseback riding, running, and pistol shooting. The sport was created to imitate the skills of a well-rounded soldier. It was introduced at the 1912 Olympic Games.

In Olympic competition, pentathletes complete all five sports in a single day! They fence, swim, and horseback ride first. Their scores determine their starting times for a final race.

For the final race, athletes run and shoot. The runners stop three times to shoot at five targets. They have to hit them all before they can run. Otherwise, they have to wait a full 70 seconds before running.

Until recently, pentathletes used air pistols to fire at targets. Then in 2010, the rules changed. Now, laser pistols are used instead. Without the use of bullets, these athletes can compete in more places than before. And, they can compete more safely.

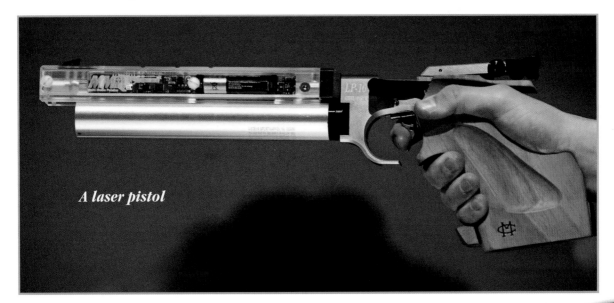

A laser pistol

Targeting the Past

Many gun sports **simulate** historical or practical skills. One popular example is cowboy action shooting.

Several organizations oversee this sport. But the main rules are the same. Shooters must use **antique** or **replica** weapons from the Old West. They also must wear cowboy costumes and use Old West names.

In cowboy hats and boots, shooters compete in timed events called stages. A stage might involve firing at targets from a stagecoach. Shooters might use an old Colt revolver or Winchester rifle.

Like all gun sports, cowboy action shooting focuses on safety. Along with their cowboy hats, shooters must wear safety glasses. Hearing protection is also highly recommended.

Fans enjoy seeing history come to life at cowboy action matches.

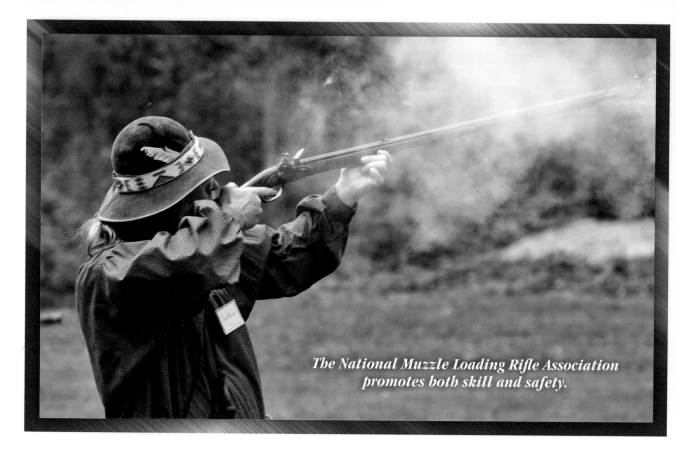

The National Muzzle Loading Rifle Association promotes both skill and safety.

Judges observe each shooter's gun handling and loading for safe practices. In fact, there are time penalties for breaking safety rules.

Other target-shooting groups also honor historical **techniques**. The National **Muzzle** Loading Rifle Association is one well-known group. It organizes events in which shooters use old-fashioned rifles. Competitors load powder and lead balls into the **muzzles** of their guns. These guns produce a lot of noise and smoke when fired!

Many people also enjoy practical shooting sports. Some practical shooting events allow only inexpensive, practical equipment. At these events, people practice self-defense instead of participating in sporting competition. The International Defensive Pistol Association oversees this kind of match.

No two International Practical Shooting Confederation courses are ever the same. This keeps the sport challenging.

The International Practical Shooting Confederation oversees events with challenging courses. Shooters may be scored for speed while running through obstacle courses. They might shoot at moving targets or from awkward positions. Each of these options adds to the variety of gun sports available for people to try.

The BRASS method is one way shooters work to improve their success on the range.

No matter which shooting sport you like best, practice is very important. Safe shooting requires you to be strong and calm. Most important, you must have knowledge of your equipment. Many local shooting clubs offer **clinics** where you can practice.

Good sportsmen know how to clean and reload their guns. Keeping weapons free of **obstructions** reduces the risk of accidents. Proper gun care differs from weapon to weapon. Learning a new sport means becoming familiar with new guns.

Learning proper breathing methods is also important in shooting sports. The BRASS method reminds shooters what to focus on. The letters stand for Breath, Relax, Aim, Squeeze, and Shot.

Breath control means holding your breath

Knowing how to properly care for your gun is an important part of gun safety. This is true for everyone from beginners to soldiers.

slightly while shooting. That way, your aim doesn't falter as you inhale or exhale. But don't hold your breath for too long! This can reduce your focus.

Hand-eye coordination is important, too. This means matching your aim with where you're looking. It's affected by how you stand and hold a gun. These are called stance and grip. Practicing them improves your **posture** and concentration. Participating in shooting sports builds **confidence**. This is helpful even off the range!

GLOSSARY

antique (an-TEEK) - an old item.

clinic - a group meeting held for the purpose of gaining specific skills or knowledge.

confidence - faith in oneself and one's powers.

marksmanship - the skill of shooting a target.

muzzle - the open front end of the barrel of a weapon.

obstruction - something that blocks something else from passing through.

posture (PAHS-chuhr) - the position or the way of holding the body.

prone - lying flat or face down.

random - lacking a definite plan or pattern.

replica - an exact copy.

silhouette (sih-luh-WEHT) - a dark outline seen against a lighter background.

simulate - to imitate.

technique (tehk-NEEK) - a method or style in which something is done.

trigger - the small lever pulled back by the finger to fire a gun.

WEB SITES

To learn more about gun sports, visit ABDO Publishing Company online. Web sites about gun sports are featured on our Book Links page. These links are routinely monitored and updated to provide the most current information available.

www.abdopublishing.com

INDEX

B
biathlon 20, 21, 22
BRASS method 29
bullet 8, 23

C
clay pigeon 7, 9, 16, 17, 18, 19
cowboy action shooting 24, 26

H
history 6, 7, 20, 22, 24, 26
hunting 7

I
International Confederation of Fullbore Rifle Associations 15
International Defensive Pistol Association 27
International Practical Shooting Confederation 27

M
marksmanship 6
modern pentathlon 22, 23
musket 6

N
National Muzzle Loading Rifle Association 26

O
Oakley, Annie 7
Olympic Games 7, 12, 14, 15, 17, 19, 22, 23

P
pistol 7, 8, 9, 12, 14, 22, 23

R
revolver 24
rifle 4, 5, 6, 7, 8, 9, 12, 14, 20, 21, 24, 26, 27

S
safety gear 5, 10, 11, 24
shooting range 4, 5, 8, 9, 10
shotgun 7, 8, 9, 16, 18, 19
skeet shooting 16, 18
sporting clays 16, 18, 19

T
target 4, 5, 6, 8, 9, 12, 14, 15, 16, 17, 18, 19, 21, 23, 24, 26, 27
trapshooting 7, 9, 16, 17, 18

U
US Long Range Rifle Teams 15
USA Shooting 12